Mechanics

Laura K. Murray

CREATIVE EDUCATION • CREATIVE PAPERBACKS

seedlings

Published by Creative Education and Creative Paperbacks
P.O. Box 227, Mankato, Minnesota 56002
Creative Education and Creative Paperbacks
are imprints of The Creative Company
www.thecreativecompany.us

Design by Ellen Huber
Production by Grant Gould
Art direction by Rita Marshall
Printed in the United States of America

Photographs by Alamy (Antonio Guillem Fernandez),
iStockphoto (anilakkus, Valerii Apetroaiei, Goodluz, Krasyuk,
SaevichMikalai, EvgeniyShkolenko, Sjoerd van der Wal,
zgurdonmaz), Shutterstock (Steve Bower, Roman Chazov,
Aleksandar Grozdanovski, Antonio Guillem, J. Lekavicius,
kurhan, Memory Stockphoto, Monkey Business Images, New
Africa, Zdenek Rosenthaler, Syda Productions, Twinsterphoto)

ISBN 9781640264144 (library binding)
ISBN 9781628329476 (paperback)
ISBN 9781640005785 (eBook)

LCCN 2020907014

TABLE OF CONTENTS

Hello, mechanics

Mechanics fix machines. They fix cars, trucks, and more. They make sure **vehicles** run safely.

Mechanics work in a repair shop. Some are part of **pit crews**.

They work
on race cars.

Mechanics work
on motorcycles.
They work
on trains and
tractors.

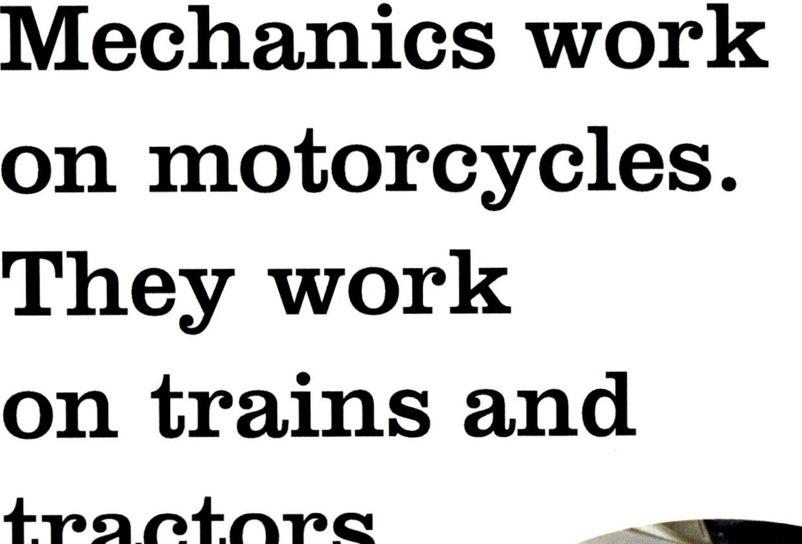

They work on planes
and boats, too.

Mechanics take care of all car parts. They look at the engine.

They check lights and belts. They fix the **brakes**.

Mechanics use
many tools.
A lift puts the
car in the air.

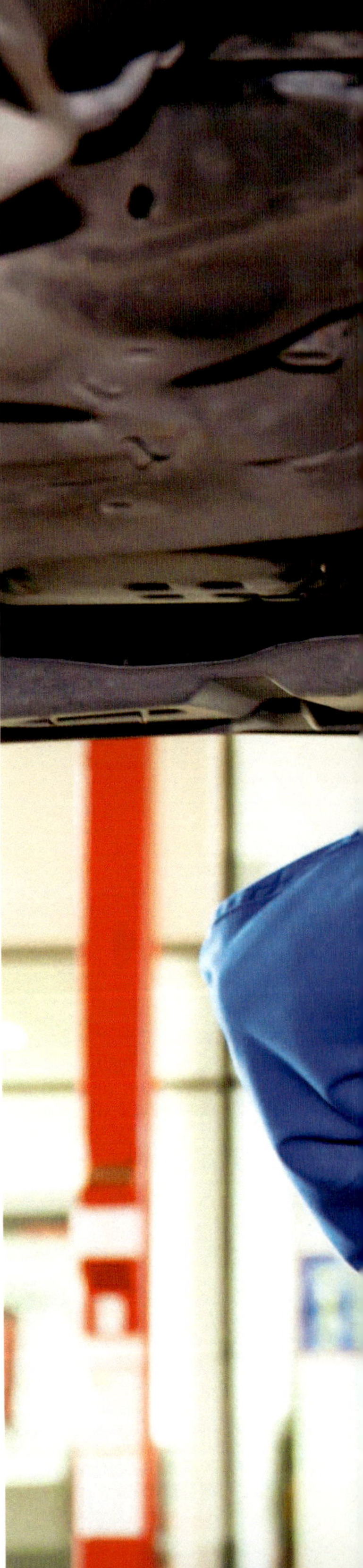

Then they can see underneath.

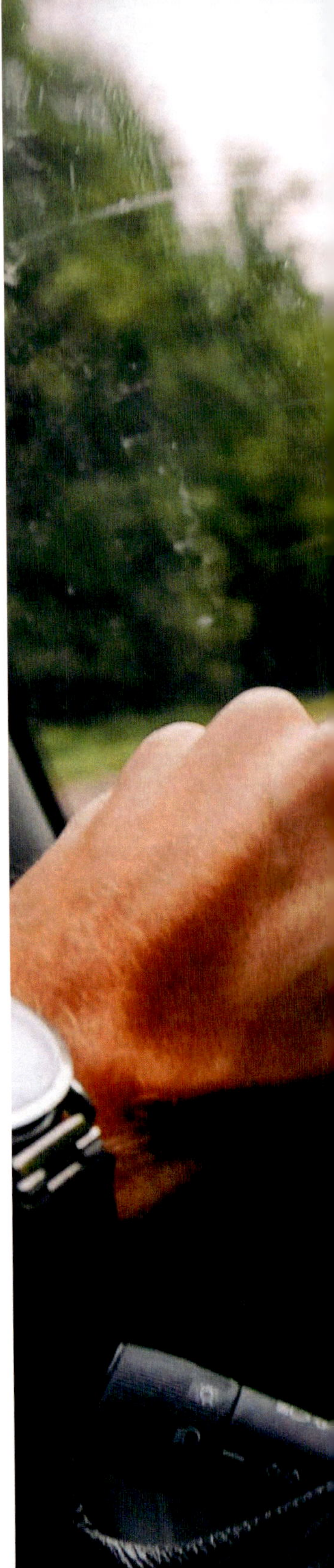

Mechanics replace tires. They change the oil.

They help people drive safely.

Thank you,
mechanics!

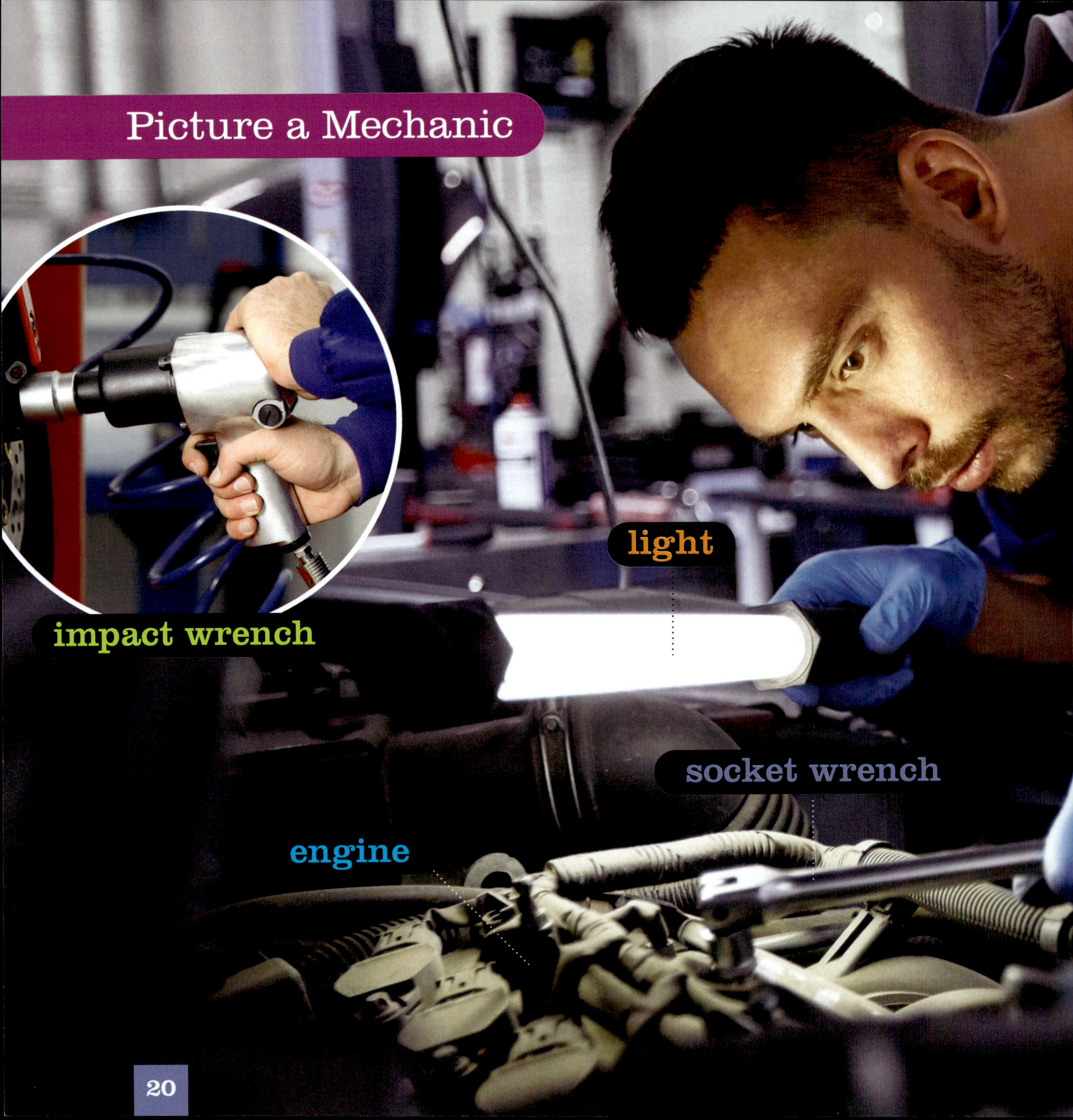

Picture a Mechanic
impact wrench
light
socket wrench
engine
20

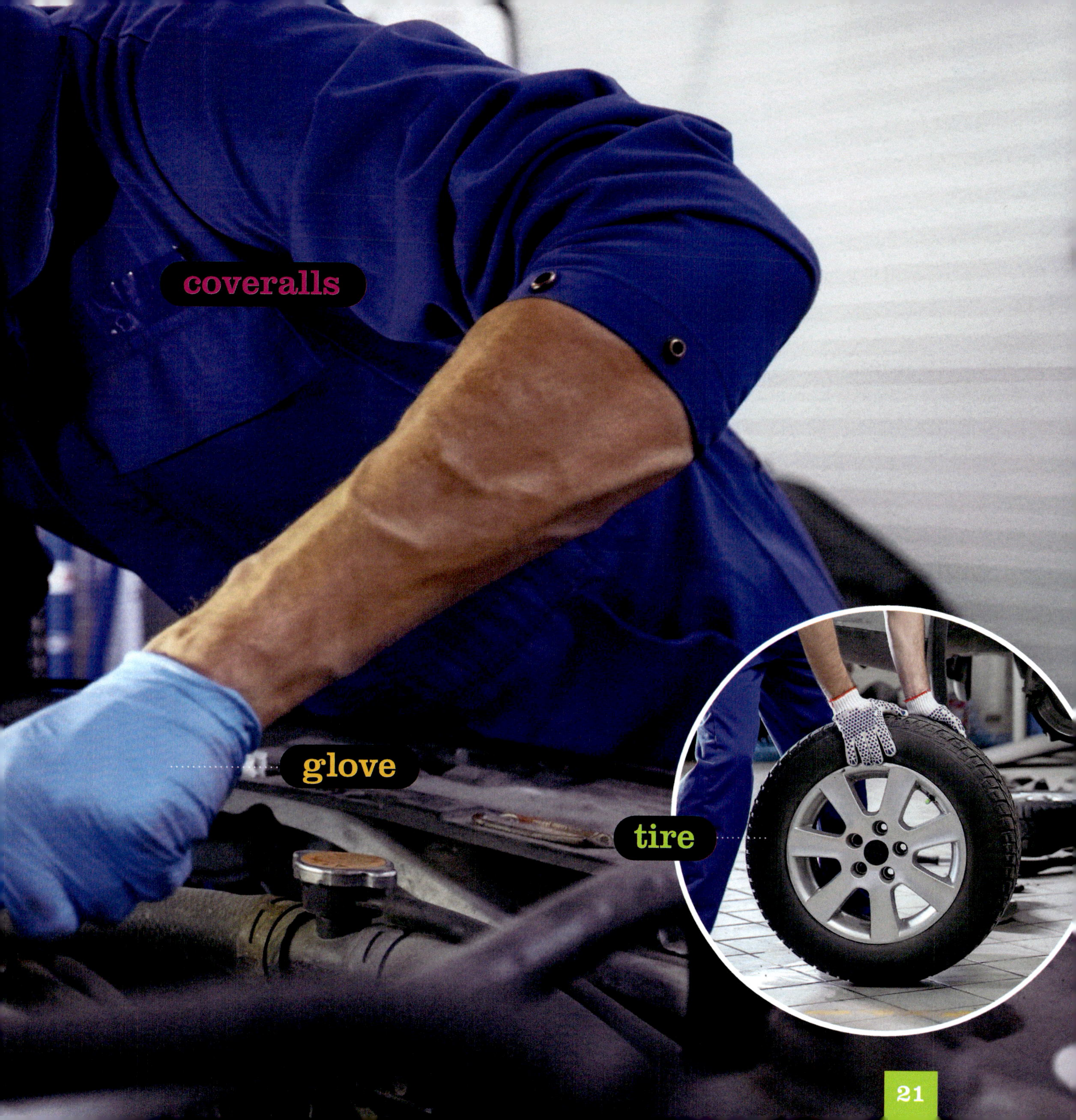

coveralls
glove
tire

brakes: parts that slow down or stop a car

engine: a machine that gives power to make something go

pit crews: teams that work on a car during a race

vehicles: things that move people or things

Honders, Christine. *What's It Really Like to Be a Mechanic?*
New York: PowerKids Press, 2019.

Leaf, Christina. *Mechanics.*
Minneapolis: Bellwether Media, 2019.

Websites

Car Mechanic Coloring Page
http://www.supercoloring.com/coloring-pages/car-mechanic

Race Car Game
https://pbskids.org/peg/games/race-car

Index